Usborne

Pocket

doodling
and
colouring
book

Designed and illustrated by Non Figg
Written by Fiona Watt
Cover designed by Erica Harrison

Doodle more houses to fill the streets...

...and add trees and fences, too.

Finish off the
pattern and
colour it in.

Draw lots more fish between the waves.

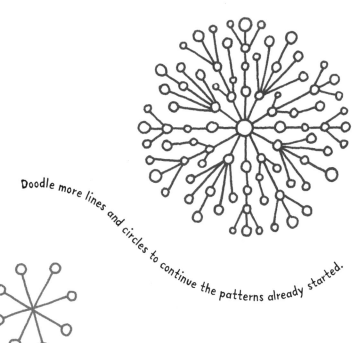

Doodle more lines and circles to continue the patterns already started.

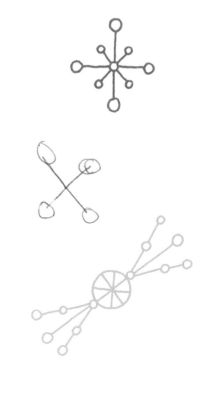

Finish off patterns on this page.

10

Doodle your own patterns on this side.

Doodle more mosquitoes until you have a huge swarm.

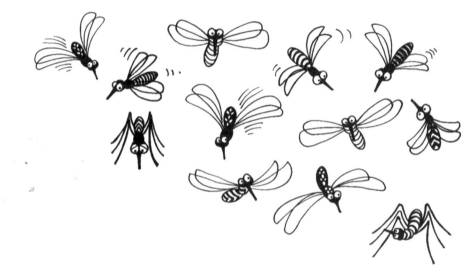

Add colour.

Maybe draw some little bugs?

14

15

Doodle birds on the wires.

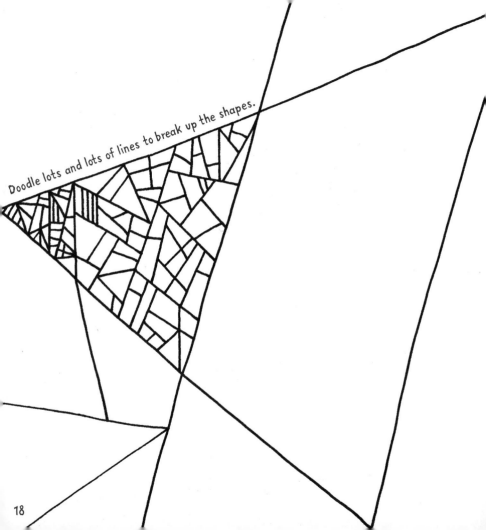

Doodle lots and lots of lines to break up the shapes.

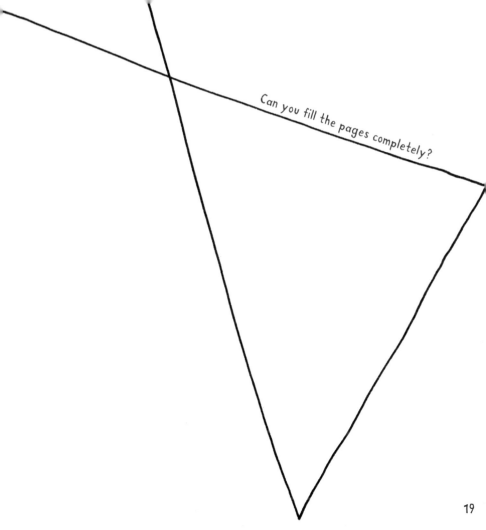

Can you fill the pages completely?

19

Continue the pattern by adding lots of curved shapes.

21

Make these shapes into faces.

Do different expressions.

Maybe glum

Surprised?

Happy!

23

Doodle patterns on the turtles.

25

Draw lines, taking
them under or over
each other.

Doodle lots of fancy feathers.

28

Doodle patterns...

Doodle patterns...

31

Draw more radio masts.

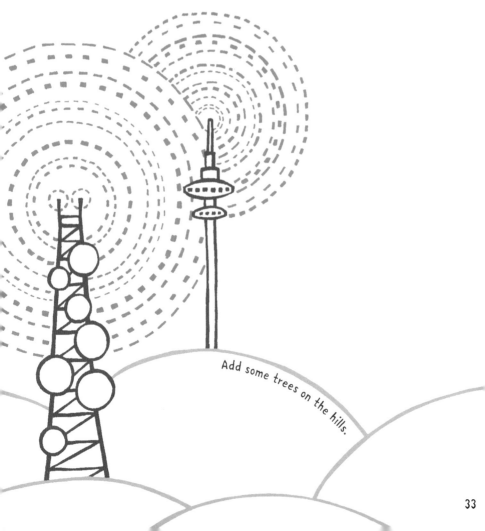

Add some trees on the hills.

33

Turn the spirals into snails' shells...

34

...decorate the shells.

Continue the pattern by doodling shapes and lines.

38

Doodle more sporty people.

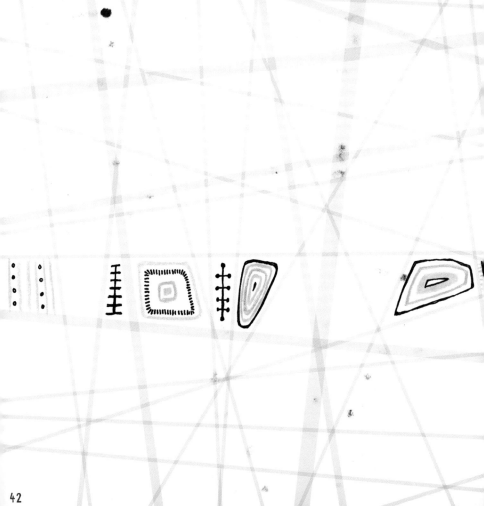

Fill the spaces
with doodles.

Doodle delicate patterns on these dandelion heads.

Doodle more fish and add lots of bubbles.

Decorate the T-shirts and add some more.

Doodle more circles with patterns.

Can you fill the pages?

51

Use the lines to make geometric patterns.

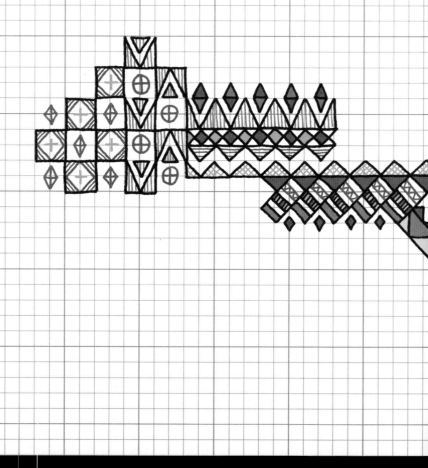

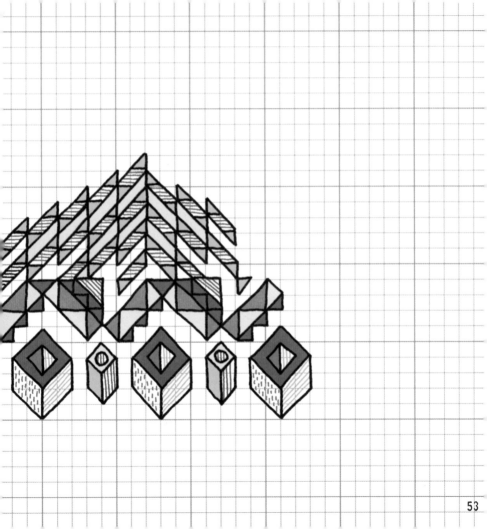

Give each thing a face.

Draw faces in the shapes to show people having fun in the waves.

Draw your own wavy line with people too, if you like.

Add more swirly lines to fill the pages.

Doodle more action figures leaping across the pages.

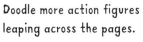

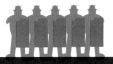

Add some hiding, too.

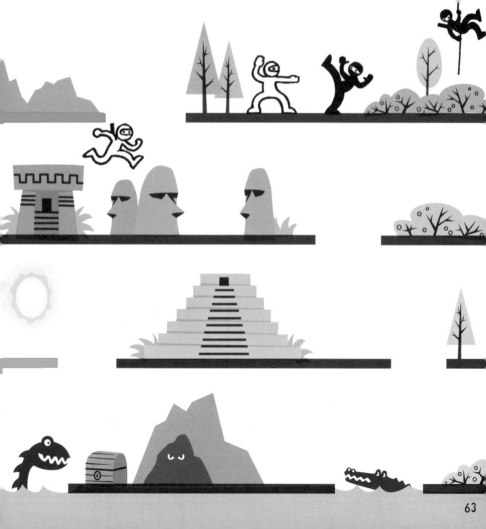

63

Draw more buildings to create a city.

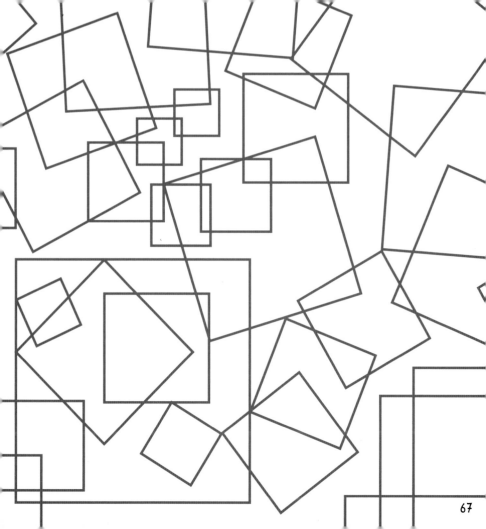

Doodle spikes on the shapes to
turn them into hedgehogs.

Add eyes and
noses, too.

Doodle the pattern without taking
your pen off the page.

Start a new pattern on this page.
Don't even take your pen off once!

Each fingerprint could become a face, animal, monster or anything else you can think of.

Doodle faces on these people.

Add more people to make a big crowd.

Carry on the doodle.

Decorate the flowers...

...and maybe add some leaves or bees?

Add more giant waves...

...and tiny boats.

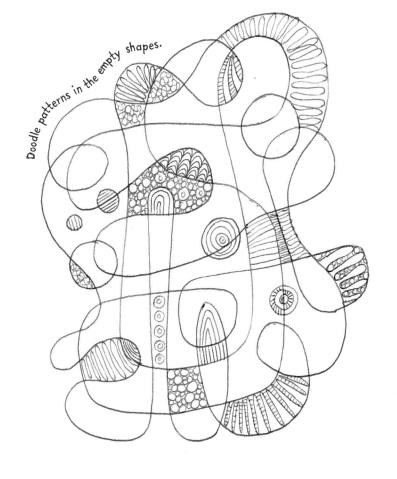

Doodle patterns in the empty shapes.

Fill this page with more looping lines and patterns.

Doodle more arrows...

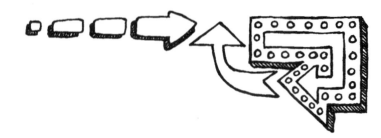

...and then some more.

Decorate the circles
in any way you like.

88

Continue the doodle to fill the pages with curvy designs.

Decorate these cakes and doughnuts.

Doodle more triangles and
fill them with faces.

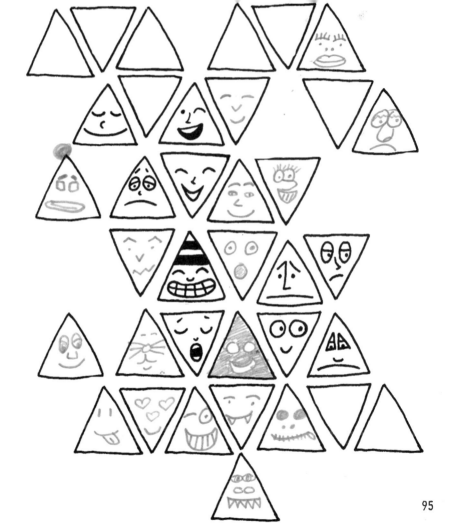

Turn these shapes into people...

...animals...

96

...monsters...

...or something else.

Draw more hearts and stars...

...and loopy star trails.

Doodle patterns along the snakes.

100

Add some forked tongues.

Fill the pages with robots.

Decorate these spirals.

Use lots of bright colours.

Doodle patterns on the shells and add snail trails.

107

Fill the pages with leaves and bugs.

Doodle more skydivers.

Add some birds, trees
and flowers, perhaps?

Now fill this side...

Carry on the pattern,
then colour it in.

Continue the patterns...

...and add lots more of your own.

Fill the shapes with windows
to turn them into buildings.

Create a world by doodling things around these planets.

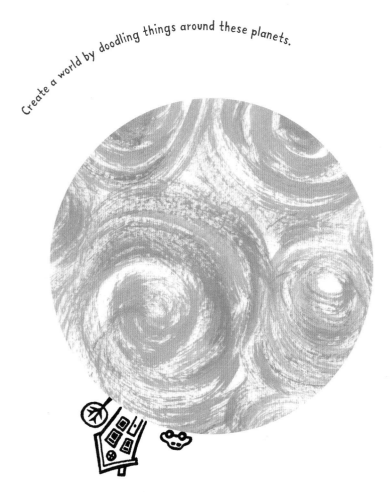

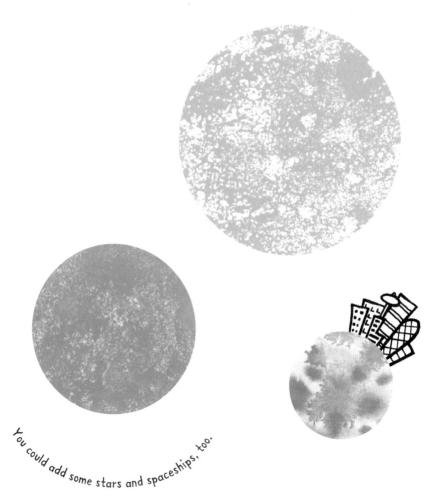

You could add some stars and spaceships, too.

123

Draw more birds...

...and more birds.

Fill the pages with patterns like these.

Fill them in with
bright colours.